関根路代・廣田純子
山中章子・吉田　要
共　著

Step by Step
～英語ワークブック～

学術図書出版社

まえがき

　このワークブックは英語初級〜中級の大学生を念頭に置いて書かれています。中学、高校で学んだ英語の見直しと、大学生として修得しておきたいボキャブラリーの確認が簡単にできるようになっています。1レッスン当たりの問題量はそれほど多くないですし、レッスンの数も12までに抑えてありますから、自学自習もやりやすいでしょう。1日に1レッスンずつ進めると、2週間ですべてを終えることができます。2レッスンずつ進めると、1週間で終えることができますね。

　もう少し細かく見てみましょう。本書は3レッスンでひとつのまとまりを構成しています。3レッスンのうちはじめの2レッスンでは、左側のページがボキャブラリーを増強するためのセクション、右側のページが文法の基礎を見直すセクションとなっています。3レッスン目ではReview として適度な分量の英文を用意しました。Review では、すでに扱われたボキャブラリーや文法事項に関する問題に加え、英文の内容理解をはかる問題が用意されています。こうして3レッスンでひとつのまとまりが構成され、それが 4 回繰り返されることで、全体で12レッスンとなります。

　12のレッスンを挟む形で、辞書の使用方法に関するページを設けました。電子辞書でもオンライン辞書でも、多くの情報を効率よく把握する一助となるでしょう。ボキャブラリーのページで書き込む意味は品詞と深い関係がありますので、「英和辞書の使い方」はぜひ参考にしてください。また、各 Review のあとには、英語にまつわるコラムをしつらえました。英語に触れる、英語を読む、英語を理解する際のヒントにしてください。

　本書が大学における英語の授業で必要とされるボキャブラリーの土台を固めること、文法事項の基礎を学び直すデザインとなっていることはすでに述べました。とりわけ大学生としてみなさんに力を入れていただきたいのは、ボキャブラリーです。ボキャブラリーと英語の理解は比例すると言っても過言ではありません。各レッスンに収められているボキャブラリーに、本書で扱われているほかの重要単語を加えた「100 Vocabulary List」も巻末に掲載しています。大学生の早い時期に、このリストを制覇する人が一人でも多く出ることを願っています。そして、ここを出発点として、さらにボキャブラリーの数を増やしていってください。

2023 年 8 月
著者一同

目次

英和辞書の使い方

　意味の分からない単語や表現が出てきたら辞書を引いてみましょう。ここでは、英和辞書の使い方を説明します。みなさんが使う辞書は何ですか？　自分の辞書の特徴も確認しましょう。

重要！ 辞書を引くときは、【品詞】と【意味】を確認しよう。

Step 1 英和辞書で"technology"を引いてみよう！
"technology"を引いてみるとこのように出てきます。

> 余裕があれば、「その他の情報」も確認してね！

☆『ジーニアス英和辞典』（第6版、南出康世・中邑光男編、2022年）参照

---

tech·nol·o·gy / tekná:lədʒi

名　（複-gies/-z/）① U C 科学技術、テクノロジー；工学；科学技術的方法

　　　　　　　　　　例　　　　文

～～～～～～～～～～～～省～～～～～略～～～～～～～～～～～～

② U C （集合的に）科学技術機器

～～～～～～～～～～～～省～～～～～略～～～～～～～～～～～～

・ 名 ←【品詞】 名は「名詞」の略。**重要！**

> どの意味があうか吟味してね！

・ 科学技術、テクノロジー；工学；科学技術的方法、科学技術機器 ←【意味】重要！

・ U C ←その他の情報　U は uncountable noun の略　（数えられない名詞）

　　　　　　　　　　　　C は countable noun の略　（数えられる名詞）

さらに、複数の形（複-gies）や発音記号（tekná:lədʒi）も書いてありますね。発音記号については19ページで説明します。

辞書の情報をもとにメモをつくってみよう。【品詞】と【意味】は必ず入れよう！

Step 2 自分の辞書で"technology"を引いてみよう!

みなさんの辞書にはどのように書かれていますか? メモしてみましょう。

> 辞書の例文や面白いと思った表現を写したり、
> 自作の例文をつくるのもいいね!

notes

品詞とは・・・単語の分類・種類のこと

名 ＝「名 詞」(n)・・・・ 人、物、事などの名前。主語や目的語になる。

動 ＝「動 詞」(v)・・・・ 人、物、事の動作・状態を示す単語。

代 ＝「代名詞」(pron)・・ 名詞の言い換えの単語。

前 ＝「前置詞」(prep)・・ 名詞や代名詞の前に置き、それらの位置を示す単語。

形 ＝「形容詞」(adj)・・・ 名詞に細かく説明を加える単語。

副 ＝「副 詞」(adv)・・・動詞、形容詞、副詞、句、節、文全体に説明を加える単語。only、even、quite など例外的に名詞に付く副詞もある。

接 ＝「接続詞」(conj)・・ 文と文、単語と単語をつなぐ単語。

助 ＝「助動詞」(v auxil)・ 動詞を助け、意味を添える単語。動詞の前に置く。

Lesson 1

Vocabulary

☆指定の品詞にあう意味を調べて、カッコに書きましょう。

advance	名　詞	（ ）
consider	動　詞	（ ）
contain	動　詞	（ ）
device	名　詞	（ ）
find	動　詞	（ ）
invent	動　詞	（ ）
modify	動　詞	（ ）

☆下の選択肢から下線にあてはまる単語を選んで入れましょう。

1. Our school _____ the website design every year.

2. He _____ himself a strong person.

3. Robots are mechanical _____ that operate automatically.

4. Johannes Gutenberg _____ the printing press in the 15th century.

5. I _____ a new Chinese restaurant near the school.

6. This drink doesn't _____ any alcohol.

7. We will experience further rapid technological _____ with AI in the future.

advances   considers   contain   devices
found   invented   modifies

主語に対する動詞

英語の文は「主語」＋「動詞」を中心に成り立っています。

Ex. I read a newspaper every morning.
　　S　V

（私は、毎朝、新聞を読みます。）

「主語」 = 〜は・が
「動詞」 = 〜する

主語 (S) + 動詞 (V) である「私は」＋「読みます」を最初に置き、そのあとに補足説明が続きます。

Exercise 1

主語に対する動詞を探し、四角で囲みましょう。

1. She began her career as an assistant movie director.

2. These dogs require a lot of care and attention.

3. The pencil is one of the most famous inventions.

4. We often take the convenience of modern technology for granted.

動詞には、「一般動詞」（〜する）と「be 動詞」（いる・ある、イコール）があります。

Exercise 2

主語に下線を引き、動詞は四角で囲みましょう。

1. The company manufactures a new line of electric cars.

2. This factory produces microchips.

3. We have many different types of video games.

4. My friends and I discovered this beach.

主語は一 語とは限らないよ。

ポイント!
主語は基本、動詞の前におくよ! 最初に動詞を探してから主語を探してもいいね。

Lesson 2

Vocabulary

☆指定の品詞にあう意味を調べて、カッコに書きましょう。

annually	副　詞	(	)
call	動　詞	(	)
compete	動　詞	(	)
defeat	動　詞	(	)
distance	名　詞	(	)
exhaustion	名　詞	(	)
prepare	動　詞	(	)

☆下の選択肢から下線にあてはまる単語を選んで入れましょう。

1. What is the _____ between Tokyo and Osaka?

2. Everybody _____ each other by their last names in my elementary school.

3. I will _____ for the exam tomorrow and stay home tonight.

4. He fell down with _____.

5. My friend pays the subscription fee _____.

6. Japanese car companies _____ with foreign companies for a share of the electric vehicle market.

7. They _____ the champion team in five sets last year.

annually	called	compete	defeated
distance	exhaustion	prepare	

時制（現在・過去・未来）

動詞は、現在・過去・未来など「時」を表すために形を変える必要があります。

時制	意味	例 ※下線は時間を表す目印	説明
現在	～する ～である	・We **have** four classes <u>on</u> Mondays. ・The sun **rises** in the east.	・毎週月曜日に授業が４つあるのは「現在の習慣」 →現在形 ・太陽は東から昇るというのは「一般的な事実」 →現在形
過去	～した ～だった	・My brother **bought** this car <u>last year</u>.	・昨年この車を買ったのは「過去の出来事」 →過去形
未来 (will)	～だろう ～するよ	・It **will rain** <u>tomorrow</u>. ・I **will clean** my room <u>this weekend</u>.	・明日雨が降るだろうと「予測」 →will ・今週末に部屋の掃除をするという「意思」 →will

《Point》時を表す目印に注目すると、どの時制の文なのかが分かりやすくなるよ！
次の Exercise では、時を表す目印を見つけてから答えを導き出そう。

Exercise 1

カッコ内の語を適する形に変えて下線に書きましょう。形を変える必要のない語もあります。

1. My sister will _____ a new smartphone tomorrow. （buy）

2. China _____ the Olympic Games in 2021. （host）

3. About 60 percent of the students _____ to school by train. （come）

4. The Tokyo Marathon _____ an annual marathon sporting event in Tokyo. （be）

Exercise 2

各文において時制の間違いを探し、正しましょう。
Ex. I ~~helped~~ you next week.
　　　→ will help

1. Today, people will use the Internet to get all kinds of information.

2. I was twenty in two years.

3. We study English together last night.

4. The garbage collectors collected the trash three times a week in my neighborhood.

Lesson 3

Review

☆英文を読み、下の問いに答えましょう。

　　　Steve Jobs (1) a pioneer in the world of technology and design. During his early years, <u>he attended a calligraphy class at college,</u>(2) even though he didn't have to. He (3) about different styles of lettering in the class. The knowledge did not seem helpful in making computers back then, but it later helped to create digital fonts for computers. His company developed many fonts on its computers. Thanks to what Jobs learned in the calligraphy class, we have access to many fonts on computers now.

　　　Keep an open mind and learn, even if the subject isn't directly related to your major. Maybe you (4) many classes in different fields at college. You never know when the knowledge or skills may become valuable in the future.

(1)　カッコにあてはまる最も適当な動詞を選びましょう。
　　　1. were　　2. have　　3. took　　4. was

(2)　主語に対する動詞を選びましょう。
　　　1. he　　2. attended　　3. a calligraphy class　　4. at college

(3)　カッコにあてはまる最も適当な動詞を選びましょう。
　　　1. will learn　　2. learns　　3. learn　　4. learned

(4)　カッコにあてはまる最も適当な動詞を選びましょう。
　　　1. will take　　2. takes　　3. will takes　　4. took

(5)　内容として正しいものを選びましょう。
　　　1. Jobs was an innovator in the field of technology and design.
　　　2. Jobs went to college after he made computers at his company.
　　　3. Job's knowledge of mathematics helped him create digital fonts for computers.

be 動詞と助動詞（動詞のお助け係）

ここでは、be 動詞と助動詞についていくつか紹介します。

be 動詞

be 動詞は実質的な意味をもたない動詞です。あえて意味をもたせるなら、「いる・ある」と「イコール（＝）」です。

John [is] in his room.
ジョンは いる　彼の部屋に

I [am] a student.
私は イコール　学生

> この文では am は「イコール」で、
> I am a student.は「私＝学生」になっているよ。

主語と be 動詞との関係

主語（〜は・が）	現在形	過去形
I	am	was
You, We They Haruka and Teru	are	were
その他（I と You 以外の単数）	is	was

Lesson 10 の受動態でも be 動詞を使うよ。
主語に合わせた be 動詞の形を確認する際は、上の表を参考に！

助動詞

動詞と一緒に用い、動詞にいろいろな意味を添えたりできる語を助動詞といいます。

助動詞	代表的な意味	例
will	〜だろう、〜するよ	I will consider it again.（意思）
should	〜すべきだ	You should be more careful with your money.（アドバイス）
can	〜できる	Aki can speak Spanish.（能力） I can meet you at 10 o'clock.（可能性）
must	〜しなければならない	We must pay taxes.（義務）

> 助動詞は動詞のお助け係で、動詞の前に置くよ！ 助動詞のあとの動詞は原型になるよ。

Lesson 4

Vocabulary

☆指定の品詞にあう意味を調べて、カッコに書きましょう。

allow	動　詞	（　　　　　　　　　　　　　　　　　　）
ancient	形容詞	（　　　　　　　　　　　　　　　　　　）
consume	動　詞	（　　　　　　　　　　　　　　　　　　）
exciting	形容詞	（　　　　　　　　　　　　　　　　　　）
quickly	副　詞	（　　　　　　　　　　　　　　　　　　）
replace	動　詞	（　　　　　　　　　　　　　　　　　　）
wooden	形容詞	（　　　　　　　　　　　　　　　　　　）

☆下の選択肢から下線にあてはまる単語を選んで入れましょう。

1. The big car your sister gave me _____ a lot of gas.

2. That temple is the oldest _____ architecture in this region.

3. The plans for exploring Mars are really _____.

4. I want to change my schedule, but my boss won't _____ it.

5. We _____ our oil heating with gas last winter.

6. The people in the valley still practice the _____ customs of their ancestors.

7. The latest news says the world's population is growing _____.

allow	ancient	consumes	exciting
quickly	replaced	wooden	

代名詞

名詞の繰り返しを避けるために**代名詞**を使います。

> burgers が they に
> 置き換わってるね!

Ex. I love [burgers], but they are not healthy.

　　(ハンバーガーが大好きだけれど、健康的ではないよね。)

代名詞の表をマスターしよう！！

単数	主格 ～は・が	所有格 ～の	目的格 ～に・を	複数	主格 ～は・が	所有格 ～の	目的格 ～に・を
私	I	my	me	私たち	we	our	us
あなた	you	your	you	あなたたち	you	your	you
彼女	she	her	her	彼女ら	they	their	them
彼	he	his	him	彼ら			
それ	it	its	it	それら			

Exercise 1

上の例のように下線の代名詞が指すものを文中から選び、四角で囲みましょう。

1. I met Jun's brother yesterday. Do you know him?

2. Kei and I are planning to go on a trip to Italy. Will you come with us?

3. Sumire is taller than her mother.

4. My children like the toys, and they were sold at that toy store.

Exercise 2

意味が通るように下線に代名詞を入れましょう。

1. This is a great movie. I like _____.

2. Yuka's parents live in Tokyo. She calls _____ every Monday.

3. Hi, Rui! What's _____ plan for tomorrow?

4. We're talking to you. Please listen to _____.

Lesson 5

Vocabulary

☆指定の品詞にあう意味を調べて、カッコに書きましょう。

during	前置詞	(	)
estimate	動　詞	(	)
figure	名　詞	(	)
justify	動　詞	(	)
survey	名　詞	(	)
system	名　詞	(	)
technical	形容詞	(	)

☆下の選択肢から下線にあてはまる単語を選んで入れましょう。

1. Do you feel a recent surge of _____ innovation?

2. The _____ show the global market for VR gaming is growing.

3. Some of my friends have an alarm _____ in the house.

4. Students can contact teachers _____ office hours.

5. The end _____ the means.

6. A _____ shows many children like to play with toys while bathing.

7. The company _____ that the construction will take five years.

during	estimates	figures	justifies
	survey	system	technical

Exercise 1

代名詞の表を完成させましょう。

単数	主格※ 〜は・が	所有格 〜の	目的格※※ 〜に・を	複数	主格※ 〜は・が	所有格 〜の	目的格※※ 〜に・を
私				私たち			
あなた				あなたたち			
彼女				彼女ら			
彼				彼ら			
それ				それら			

※主格は文中で主語の役割を果たす。※※目的格は文中で目的語の役割を果たす。

Exercise 2

下線を代名詞に置き換えましょう。

Ex. Fine feathers make <u>fine birds</u>. 「馬子にも衣裳」 （　them　）

> 考え方！　fine birds は複数で、動詞 make の目的語なので、them（それら）になる。

1. The teacher gave <u>Yuko and me</u> books and pictures. （　　　　　）

2. <u>Music</u> gives people pleasure. （　　　　　）

3. We will have a party to celebrate <u>Ken's</u> fifth birthday. （　　　　　）

4. <u>Her sister</u> bought me a watch. （　　　　　）

> **Attention!　代名詞を選ぶときは文の意味を大切に！**
>
> 下線に入る代名詞は何でしょう？
>
> The boy frequently played ＿＿＿＿ favorite song when he became sad.
>
> 　　　a. he　　b. his　　c. him
>
> 動詞 played の目的語なので c を選びがちですが、文の意味をよく考えてみましょう。
>
> played [演奏した]＋him [彼を] favorite song [お気に入りの歌]では意味が？？
>
> <u>不自然でない</u>文の意味は「男の子は悲しくなると<u>彼の</u>お気に入りの歌をよく演奏する」です。
>
> 「彼のお気に入りの歌」なので、**答えは b!　代名詞を選ぶときは文の意味を大切に！**

Lesson 6

Review

☆英文を読み、下の問いに答えましょう。

　　The market of AI (Artificial Intelligence) robots is overgrowing. <u>As an example, we take an AI pet robot.</u>(1) People have <u>it</u>(2) because it's easier to look after, they don't need to worry about its health, and they have a genuine interest in AI, etc.

　　Incidentally, do you know a robot pet funeral held in Japan? <u>The memorial service</u>(3) has drawn attention from overseas media. They are also interested in Japanese views on robots: they are friendly to people, like in some popular anime and manga. On the other hand, robots are thought to threaten human beings, mainly by replacing <u>them</u>(4) at work in foreign countries. They are surprised at the cultural difference.

　　Then how do you want to be involved with AI or robots?

(1)　主語を選びましょう。
　　　1. As　　　2. an example　　　3. we　　　4. an AI pet robot

(2)　"it" が指すものを選びましょう。
　　　1. The market　　　2. overgrowing
　　　3. an example　　　4. an AI pet robot

(3)　"The memorial service" を代名詞に置き換えましょう。
　　　1. It　　　2. He　　　3. They　　　4. You

(4)　"them" が指すものを選びましょう。
　　　1. media　　　2. robots　　　3. human beings　　　4. foreign countries

(5)　内容として正しいものを選びましょう。
　　　1. AI lives shorter than human beings.
　　　2. A pet robot is becoming a severe problem in many countries.
　　　3. Descriptions of robots in Japan are known in foreign countries.

声に出して読んでみよう

6 ページで英和辞書の使い方を確認しましたが、その中に発音記号がありました。単語、文、文章など、英語は声に出して読んでみましょう。声に出すことで、「自分の言葉」になります。

例）technology

辞書には tech・nol・o‐gy / tekná:lədʒi とありました。

tech・nol・o‐gy ←4音節　「・」と「‐」が音節の句切れ目

tekná:lədʒi ←発音記号

英語は 15～20 の母音と 24 の子音が組み合わさっています。ここでは母音に注目してみましょう。

tek の **e**　　　日本語の「エ」のように発音

ná:l の **á:**　　a+音を伸ばす記号【:】という意味。日本語の「オ」の口で「ア」と発声さらに、a:に「′(アクセント記号)」が付いている。

※アクセント記号が付いている音を強調して読みましょう!

ə　　　　　シュワー(schwa)と呼ばれるアクセントのない母音。口をリラックスさせて、短く「ア」と発音。

dʒi の **i**　　　口を横に引きすぎずに日本語の「イ」と発音

これは一例ですが、英語と日本語では「言葉の音」が違うことに気がつきますよね。音は電子辞書やインターネットで検索して聞くことができます。

何度も声に出して「英語の音」を修得しましょう!

Lesson 7

Vocabulary

☆指定の品詞にあう意味を調べて、カッコに書きましょう。

combine	動 詞	(	)
contrast	名 詞	(	)
develop	動 詞	(	)
explain	動 詞	(	)
form	名 詞	(	)
mechanism	名 詞	(	)
refuse	動 詞	(	)

☆下の選択肢から下線にあてはまる単語を選んで入れましょう。

1. The engineer showed me the _____ of a new electronic car.
2. Ice is a solid _____ of water.
3. The blue sky is in beautiful _____ with the white snow.
4. I _____ his request to give him the answers to the homework.
5. Scientists are trying to _____ new drugs to stop the disease.
6. "Workcation" _____ work and vacation.
7. Please _____ why you were late for class.

combines	contrast	develop	explain
form	mechanism	refused	

Exercise 1

下の選択肢から各イメージ図にあう前置詞を選んでカッコに入れましょう。

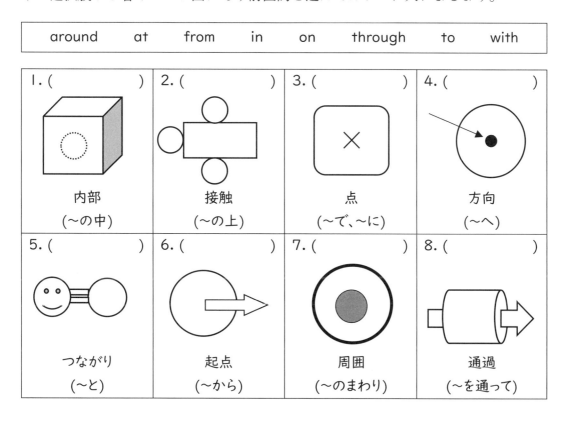

around	at	from	in	on	through	to	with

1. (   )　内部（〜の中）
2. (   )　接触（〜の上）
3. (   )　点（〜で、〜に）
4. (   )　方向（〜へ）
5. (   )　つながり（〜と）
6. (   )　起点（〜から）
7. (   )　周囲（〜のまわり）
8. (   )　通過（〜を通って）

Exercise 2

下の選択肢から下線にあてはまる前置詞を選んで入れましょう。

1. Tom is the funniest person _____ our class.

2. Hang the TV screen _____ that wall.

3. I went _____ a new robot exhibition _____ him last weekend.

4. George came _____ Australia to study _____ a Japanese university.

at	from	in	on	to	with

> 4問とも、前置詞の後ろには名詞か代名詞がきています。
> 前置詞は名詞や代名詞の「前」に「置」いて、位置情報を示す言葉なんですね。
> 前置詞と名詞や代名詞が組み合わさって、意味のかたまりをつくります。

Lesson 8

Vocabulary

☆指定の品詞にあう意味を調べて、カッコに書きましょう。

discover	動　詞	(	)
increase	動　詞	(	)
ingredient	名　詞	(	)
lower	動　詞	(	)
process	名　詞	(	)
product	名　詞	(	)
rate	名　詞	(	)

☆下の選択肢から下線にあてはまる単語を選んで入れましょう。

1. The company uses only natural _____ in its products.

2. It takes a lot of _____ to make cars.

3. It took two years to bring this new _____ to the market.

4. The graph shows that the birth _____ is not rising.

5. I have _____ the secret of continuing to learn.

6. John carefully _____ the solar panels from the roof.

7. The number of people living in the city _____ by ten percent last year.

discovered	increased	ingredients
lowered	processes	product	rate

Exercise 1

各文の下線にあてはまる副詞を下の選択肢から選んで入れましょう。大文字で使用するものも小文字で書かれています。

frequently	next	there	yesterday

1. First, check the machine for oil leaks. _____, turn on the power.

2. I went to the motor show to check out the new car line-up _____.

3. The musician _____ played the guitar in high school.

4. My friend lives in Osaka. I want to go _____ to see him.

時間
now (いま), later (あとで)
recently (最近)

場所
near (近く), far (遠く)
here (ここで、ここに)

副詞
主に動詞や文全体に情報を付け加える名脇役。語尾に ly が付くことが多いです。

頻度
always (いつも)
frequently (頻繁に)

程度
really (本当に)
almost (ほとんど)

Exercise 2

各文の下線にあてはまる副詞を下の選択肢から選んで入れましょう。大文字で使用するものも小文字で書かれています。

especially	exactly	often	rapidly

1. _____ one hundred people took part in the drone show.

2. She _____ goes to the DIY store to buy nails and screws.

3. I like swimming, _____ in the river in summer.

4. The disease spread _____ the first time, but then gradually declined.

Lesson 9

Review

☆英文を読み、下の問いに答えましょう。

　　　Connecting is a wonderful way to improve our everyday lives. Let's look (1) some examples of connecting things.

　　　One plus one is two. This is just a calculation. Then, what happens when you put two wheels (2)? They become a bicycle! Put two things together, and they take on a new form.

　　　If you mix blue (3) yellow, you get green. When you combine hydrogen and oxygen, you get H_2O. These changes tell us how two different things work together to create a new state.

　　　You can (4) more than three different things. Let's consider combining the first letters of each word — tool, electricity, cell, heat, network, oil, light, operation, gas, yard.

(1)　カッコにあてはまる最も適切なものを選びましょう。
　　　1. at　　2. in　　3. on　　4. to

(2)　カッコにあてはまる最も適切なものを選びましょう。
　　　1. first　　2. together　　3. often　　4. really

(3)　カッコにあてはまる最も適切なものを選びましょう。
　　　1. after　　2. for　　3. from　　4. with

(4)　カッコにあてはまる最も適切なものを選びましょう。
　　　1. combine　　2. refuse　　3. discover　　4. increase

(5)　最後の文の答えとして最も適切なものを選びましょう。
　　　1. water　　2. science　　3. technology　　4. ingredient

英語は語順通りに理解しよう

みなさんは Lesson 1 で、英語が**主語**と**動詞**を中心に成り立っている言語だということを確認しましたね。では主語と動詞以外の部分はどうなっているかというと、あとは説明語句が付け加わっているだけです！

> I met him at a bookstore in Shinjuku yesterday.
> （私は昨日、新宿の本屋で彼に会った。）

「私は会った」という主語・動詞に、「彼に」「新宿の本屋で」「昨日」という情報が付け足されていますね。情報の出され方を整理してみると次のようになっています。

I met	(1)「〜は・が」（主語）「〜する」（動詞）
him	(2)「誰・何に」
at a book store in Omiya	(3)「どこで」
yesterday.	(4)「いつ」

なんと、英語と日本語で情報の出され方がほぼ真逆になっています。「いつ、どこで、誰が、何をした」方式の日本語で英語を考えると、反対の方向から英語を見返すことになってしまうわけです。そんなの面倒ですね。

そこでオススメなのが、英語の語順通りに、出てきた情報から、意味のかたまりごとに、情報を仕入れていく読み方です。もう少し長めの文で見てみましょう。

> I will take the Hayabusa, / a bullet train, / from Tokyo Station /
> to Hakodate / at 10 a.m. / next Sunday.

「はやぶさに乗ります」「新幹線の」「東京駅から」「函館まで」「午前 10 時に」「来週の日曜」と語順通りに見ていけば、主語・動詞という重要な情報から始まり、付け足し部分の説明語句が続いているのが分かります。

「誰・何に」「誰・何を」、前置詞、when や that(Lesson 11 参照)、カンマ「,」などが区切れの目印です。慣れるまでは斜め線のスラッシュ「/」を入れて練習してみてください。

Lesson 10

Vocabulary

☆指定の品詞にあう意味を調べて、カッコに書きましょう。

avoid	動 詞	(　　　　　　　　　　　　　　　　　　　　　)
cause	動 詞	(　　　　　　　　　　　　　　　　　　　　　)
experience	名 詞	(　　　　　　　　　　　　　　　　　　　　　)
follow	動 詞	(　　　　　　　　　　　　　　　　　　　　　)
leave	動 詞	(　　　　　　　　　　　　　　　　　　　　　)
think	動 詞	(　　　　　　　　　　　　　　　　　　　　　)
vivid	形容詞	(　　　　　　　　　　　　　　　　　　　　　)

☆下の選択肢から下線にあてはまる単語を選んで入れましょう。

1. Baby birds _____ their parents, or the first thing they see.

2. Too much trans-fat can _____ you several diseases.

3. Albert Einstein said, "Learning is _____. Everything else is just information." So, let's try everything!

4. I usually _____ home for school at seven a.m.

5. You should _____ drinking coffee at night.

6. I _____ that studying a little every day is a nice idea.

7. Trees turn _____ red and yellow in autumn due to bright light and excess plant sugars within leaf cells.

avoid	cause	experience	
follow	leave	think	vivid

受動態

動作や変化を<u>受けた側（＝目的語）</u>を強調したいときに、受動態を使います。

Exercise 1

上の≪能動態≫の例を参考に、動詞を四角で囲い、目的語に下線を引きましょう。

動詞の過去分詞形を右の下線に書きましょう。

※動詞の過去分詞形は、55-57 ページの「動詞語形変化表」を見てみよう。

1. His vivid green hair surprised his friends.　　　_____

2. The technical trouble caused the accident.　　　_____

3. The dance party follows the ceremony.　　　_____

4. Someone broke the window yesterday.　　　_____

Exercise 2

上の≪受動態≫の例を参考に、上の問題の文章を受動態に書き換えてみましょう。

1. _____ by his vivid green hair.

2. _____ by the technical trouble.

3. _____ by the dance party.

4. _____ yesterday.

> ■ 能動態→受動態への 3 つの基本ステップ ■
>
> (1) <動詞>と<目的語>に印をつける（主語と動詞については Lesson 1）
>
> (2) <目的語>を<主語>の場所に移動。（<目的語>が新主語に！）
>
> (3) <動詞>を、新主語に合わせた<be 動詞>+動詞の<過去分詞>に変える。
>
> 　この be 動詞+過去分詞を「受動態セット」として意識しましょう。
>
> ※ 動作主に注目しなければ「by~」は使いません。

Lesson 11

Vocabulary

☆指定の品詞にあう意味を調べて、カッコに書きましょう。

attract	動 詞	(	)
compare	動 詞	(	)
describe	動 詞	(	)
empty	形容詞	(	)
fill	動 詞	(	)
improve	動 詞	(	)
several	形容詞	(	)

☆下の選択肢から下線にあてはまる単語を選んで入れましょう。

1. Can you _____ what your hometown is like?

2. These engineers will _____ the engine to reduce gas emission.

3. Please _____ my glass with water.

4. You can use the _____ container on the table for lunch.

5. Their survey results will _____ the attention of scientists from all over the world.

6. Scientists should _____ all different data.

7. The company manufactures _____ types of tools.

attract	compare	describe
empty	fill	improve several

複文

複文は、【主節】（メイン SV*）と【従属節】（サブ SV）からつくられる文のこと。

従属節は条件や原因を、主節は結果として起こることや結論を表します。

メインは主節。「文の SV」といったら主節の SV のことです!!

【主節】　　　　　【従属節】

You can go / when the traffic light turns green.
　S　　　V

（行っていいですよ / 信号が青になったら。）

《Point 1》
　従属節の目印 before, after, when, where, if などが、主節との区切れ目。

【従属節】　　　　　　　　　【主節】

When the traffic light is red, / **you must stop**.
　　　　　　　　　　　　　　　　　　S　　　　　V

（信号が赤のときは、/ 止まらないといけません。）

《Point 2》
　When など従属節の目印が文頭にあるときは、カンマ「,」が主節との区切れ目。

Exercise 1

主節と従属節の区切れ目にスラッシュ「/」を入れ、主節に下線を引きましょう。

1. Because I didn't have time, my friend kindly helped me.

2. They bought the new EV after its driving system was improved.

3. We have seven miles to go before we can take a break.

4. While the cat was sleeping on the tree, he painted its picture.

Exercise 2

主節と従属節の区切れ目にスラッシュ「/」を入れ、主節の主語に「S」、主節の動詞に「V」とメモを書きましょう。

1. I compared three smartphones because I wanted to get the best one.

2. Bob was talking on the phone when his friend suddenly opened the door.

3. If your hands are empty, will you carry this bag for me?

4. Editors checked several facts before the book was published.

Lesson 12

Review

☆英文を読み、下の問いに答えましょう。

There was a girl named Emma who loved to play sports. She tried several sports—tennis, basketball, soccer, swimming, and marathon. Her friends admired her, but she was getting bored with ordinary sports. She wanted a new experience.

One day, <u>when Emma and her friends were playing in a park, they found a frisbee.</u>(1) She picked it up and threw it. It flew through the air in a beautiful curve before landing on the ground. She felt so good.

Emma's friends were impressed with her throw, and <u>they wanted to know how far the frisbee could go.</u>(2) Every time she threw it, they measured the distance and calculated the average of her throws. She was happy to find out that her throws were getting better and better. <u>Her friends encouraged her to practice more.</u>(3)

Emma was determined to <u>improve</u>(4) her frisbee skills. She needed to predict the distance of her throws based on the height and angle of her toss and the various materials of the disc. So, she studied physics in addition to practicing throwing. Finally, she became a frisbee player who was also a physicist and impressed everyone!

(1)　文（主節）の主語を選びましょう。

　　 1. when　　2. Emma　　3. they　　4. a frisbee

(2)　文（主節）の動詞を選びましょう。

　　 1. wanted　　2. know　　3. how　　4. go

(3)　この文を、Emma を主語にした受動態に書き直しましょう。

　　 ＿＿＿＿＿＿＿＿＿＿＿＿＿＿＿＿＿ by her friends to practice more.

(4)　"improve" と同じような意味になるものを選びましょう。

　　 1. get bored　　2. impress　　3. get better　　4. predict

(5)　内容として正しいものを選びましょう。

　　 1. Emma could not throw the frisbee well at first.

　　 2. Her friends helped Emma to measure the angle of her throws.

　　 3. Emma calculated the height and angle of her toss to predict.

「パラグラフ」は思考の整理術

「書くことが苦手…」という人、安心してください。私も仲間です。

「書くことが好き！」という人、相手にもっと伝えたいですよね。

アイディアがないわけではないけれど、それを相手に伝わるように書くのは簡単ではありません。レポートなんて地獄です。でも、ぼんやりしたアイディアや心のモヤモヤを整理していくと、自己表現の手掛かりがつかめます。きっと「苦手」が（少しだけ）減ります。ここでは、そんな思考整理術として「パラグラフ」(paragraph)のヒミツを紹介します。

■「パラグラフ」って何？

日本語だと「段落」ですが、英文のパラグラフはしくみが明確。構成メンバーと役割が決まっているチームのようなもの。一つのパラグラフは、チーム一丸となって一つのトピックを伝えます。

■ パラグラフのチームメンバー

1. Topic sentence （いちばん伝えたいこと。不動のエースストライカー）
2. Supporting sentences （詳細や具体例。目配りのできる MF）
3. Concluding sentence （まとめ。GK 的チームの要）

■ Topic sentence （不動のエースストライカー）

自分の意見や結論を１文で簡潔に述べたもの。ここは絶対外せない！　読ませたい！　だからパラグラフの最初に置かれることが多いです。

■ Supporting sentences （目配りのできる MF）

Topic sentence をサポートするため、読者が想像できるような説明や具体例を提示する文。パスやディフェンスでエースをサポートします。

■ Concluding sentence （GK 的チームの要）

最後のダメ押しとして、Topic sentence の主旨をまとめ直したもの。Supporting sentences と協力してエースの仕事を盛り立てて、チーム全体＝パラグラフを一つにまとめあげます。

Lesson 12 長文の各パラグラフ構造は、解答に載せてあります。構造を確認しながら読み直してみましょう。

英英辞書の使い方

ステップアップとして、英語を英語で理解してみましょう。

重要！ 英英辞書を引くときも、【品詞】と【意味】を確認しよう。

Step 1 オンラインの英英辞書を検索してみよう！ 下記は主なサイトです。

- Longman Learner's Dictionary
- Oxford Learner's Dictionary
- Cambridge Learner's Dictionary
- Collins Online Dictionary

Step 2 英英辞書で "manufacture" を引いてみよう！

---

manufacture (mæ̀njufǽktʃər)

1. verb

  to make something in a factory, usually in large quantities
   ・They manufacture automobiles at the factory in Mexico.
   ・We import goods manufactured overseas.

2. noun [uncountable]

  the process of making goods or products in a factory
   ・the efficient methods of manufacture

・ verb, noun ← 【品詞】verb は動詞、noun は名詞。**重要！**

・ to make something in a factory, usually in large quantities ← 【意味】**重要！**

・ They manufacture automobiles at the factory in Mexico. ← 用例、例文

・ uncountable ← 不可算名詞（数えられない名詞）

各 Lesson に出てきた単語も英英辞書で調べてみましょう。

Lesson 1		
advance	n	
consider	v	
contain	v	
device	n	
find	v	
invent	v	
modify	v	

Lesson 2		
annually	adv	
call	v	
compete	v	
defeat	v	
distance	n	
exhaustion	n	
prepare	v	

Lesson 4		
allow	v	
ancient	adj	
consume	v	
exciting	adj	
quickly	adv	
replace	v	
wooden	adj	

Lesson 5		
during	prep	
estimate	v	
figure	n	
justify	v	
survey	n	
system	n	
technical	adj	

Lesson 7		
combine	v	
contrast	n	
develop	v	
explain	v	
form	n	
mechanism	n	
refuse	v	

Lesson 8		
discover	v	
increase	v	
ingredient	n	
lower	v	
process	n	
product	n	
rate	n	

Lesson 10		
avoid	v	
cause	v	
experience	n	
follow	v	
leave	v	
think	v	
vivid	adj	

Lesson 11		
attract	v	
compare	v	
describe	v	
empty	adj	
fill	v	
improve	v	
several	adj	

解 答

Lesson 1

Vocabulary

advance	名　詞	（ 進歩 ）
consider	動　詞	（ よく考える、熟考する ）
contain	動　詞	（ 含む ）
device	名　詞	（ 装置、道具 ）
find	動　詞	（ 見つける ）
invent	動　詞	（ 発明する ）
modify	動　詞	（ 修正する、改良する ）

1. modifies　　2. considers　　3. devices　　4. invented
5. found　　6. contain　　7. advances

Exercise 1

1. began　2. require　3. is　4. take

Exercise 2

1. The company manufactures　2. This factory produces
3. We have　4. My friends and I discovered

1. manufacture は「製造する」という意味の動詞。The company が三人称単数形だか
   ら、manufacture に s が付いている。
2. produce は「製造する、生産する」という意味の動詞。manufacture の類義語。
3. different types of video games は、異なる種類のテレビゲームの意味。
4. My friends and I（友人と私）が主語となっている。主語は一語とは限らない。

Lesson 2

Vocabulary

annually	副　詞	（　毎年、一年ごとに　）
call	動　詞	（　呼ぶ　）
compete	動　詞	（　競争する　）
defeat	動　詞	（　破る、負かす　）
distance	名　詞	（　距離　）
exhaustion	名　詞	（　極度の疲労　）
prepare	動　詞	（　準備する　）

１. distance　　2. called　　3. prepare　　4. exhaustion

5. annually　　6. compete　　7. defeated

Exercise 1

１. buy　　2. hosted　　3. come　　4. is

１. will（助動詞）のあとは、動詞は原型になる。

3. この学校の約 60％の学生は電車で通学しているという「現在の習慣、（この学校での）一般的な事実）」を述べているので、時制は現在形。

Exercise 2

１. will をとる　　2. was→will be　　3. study→studied　　4. collected→collect

１. 現在、人々はインターネットで情報を得ているという「一般的な事実」を述べているので、時制は現在形。

2. in two years は 2 年後の意味。未来のことを述べているので時制は未来形。

3. last night（昨夜）があるので、時制は過去形。study の過去形は、y の前の文字が d（子音）なので、y を i に変えて ed を付ける。

4. 私の地域では、ゴミ回収車が週 3 回、ゴミを集めているという「現在の習慣、（この地域での）一般的な事実」を述べているので、時制は現在形。

Lesson 3

Review

(1) 4　　(2) 2　　(3) 4　　(4) 1　　(5) 1

訳

　　スティーブ・ジョブスは、科学技術とデザインの世界の先駆者だった。若い頃、ジョブスは大学でカリグラフィー（西欧の書道）の授業に出席した、もっとも出席する必要はなかったのに。ジョブスは、その授業でカリグラフィーのいろいろな書体について学んだ。その知識は当時、コンピュータをつくるのには役立たないようにみえたが、のちにコンピュータで使用するデジタル文字の字体（フォント）をつくるのに役に立った。ジョブスがカリグラフィーの授業で学んだことによって、現在私たちは、コンピュータで多くの字体を利用できる。

　　（大学の）専門には直接関係がないような科目であっても、固定観念にとらわれず学びなさい。もしかしたら、あなたは大学で異なる分野の授業を多く履修するかもしれない。将来あなたにとって、いつその知識やスキルが役に立つのかは分からないのだ。

Lesson 4

Vocabulary

allow	動　詞	（ 許す ）
ancient	形容詞	（ 古来の、古代の ）
consume	動　詞	（ 消費する、消耗する ）
exciting	形容詞	（ 興奮させる、わくわくさせる ）
quickly	副　詞	（ 速く、急いで ）
replace	動　詞	（ 取り替える、取って代わる ）
wooden	形容詞	（ 木製の ）

1. consumes　　2. wooden　　3. exciting　　4. allow
5. replaced　　6. ancient　　7. quickly

Exercise 1

1. Jun's brother　2. Kei and I　3. Sumire　4. the toys

Exercise 2

1. it　2. them　3. your　4. us

1. a great movie が it に置き換えられている。
2. Yuka's parents が them に置き換えられている。
3. Rui は呼びかけられている対象（you）であるので、your になる。
4.「私たちはあなたに話しています。私たちの話を聞いて。」us が正解。

Lesson 5

Vocabulary

during	前置詞	（ 〜の間に ）
estimate	動　詞	（ 見積もる、概算する ）
figure	名　詞	（ 数値、数量）
justify	動　詞	（ 正しいと証明する、正当化する ）
survey	名　詞	（ 調査、査定）
system	名　詞	（ 装置、制度）
technical	形容詞	（ 工業技術の、科学技術の ）

1. technical　　2. figures　　3. system　　4. during
5. justifies　　6. survey　　7. estimates

Exercise 1

単数	主格 〜は・が	所有格 〜の	目的格 〜に・を	複数	主格 〜は・が	所有格 〜の	目的格 〜に・を
私	I	my	me	私たち	we	our	us
あなた	you	your	you	あなたたち	you	your	you
彼女	she	her	her	彼女ら			
彼	he	his	him	彼ら	they	their	them
それ	it	its	it	それら			

Exercise 2

1. us　　2. It　　3. his　　4. She

1. Yuko and me は「私」が含まれているので「私たち（複数）」になる。gave の目的語なので us が正解。
2. Music は単数で、主語なので It が正解。
3. Ken's は「ケンの」という意味。ケンは男性の名前なので his が正解。
4. Her sister「彼女の姉（妹）」は単数で、主語なので She が正解。

Lesson 6

Review

(1) 3　　(2) 4　　(3) 1　　(4) 3　　(5) 3

訳

　　AI（人工知能）ロボット市場が急速に発展している。一例として、AI ペットロボットを取り上げる。世話をするのが楽だから、健康の心配をする必要がないから、AI に純粋に興味があるからといった理由で人々は AI ペットロボットを飼う。

　　ところで、日本で行われているペットロボットの葬儀をご存じだろうか。この葬儀は、海外メディアに注目されている。彼らは、日本の一部の人気アニメや漫画に見られるように、ロボットと人が友好的な関係にあるという、日本のロボット観にも興味を示している。一方、外国では、ロボットは主に仕事を奪うという理由から、人間を脅かす存在と考えられている。彼らは日本と海外の文化の違いに驚いている。

　　では、あなたは AI やロボットとどのように関わっていきたい？

Lesson 7

Vocabulary

combine	動　詞	（ 結合させる、組み合わせる ）
contrast	名　詞	（ 対照、対比 ）
develop	動　詞	（ 発達させる、発展させる ）
explain	動　詞	（ 説明する ）
form	名　詞	（ 形、姿 ）
mechanism	名　詞	（ 機械装置、仕組み ）
refuse	動　詞	（ 断る、拒絶する ）

1. mechanism　　2. form　　　3. contrast　　　4. refused
5. develop　　　6. combines　　7. explain

Exercise 1

1. in　　2. on　　3. at　　　4. to
5. with　6. from　7. around　8. through

Exercise 2

1. in　　2. on　　3. to, with　　4. from, at

1. クラスの「中で」。「クラス」が箱のイメージ。
2. テレビのスクリーンを壁に接触させるイメージ。
3. ロボットの展示「に」行ったという方向。彼「と(一緒に)」。
4. オーストラリア「から」やって来て、日本の大学「で」学ぶ。

Lesson 8

Vocabulary

discover	動　詞	（ 発見する ）
increase	動　詞	（ 増える ）
ingredient	名　詞	（ 成分、材料 ）
lower	動　詞	（ 下げる、おろす ）
process	名　詞	（ 過程、工程 ）
product	名　詞	（ 製品、生産物 ）
rate	名　詞	（ 率、割合 ）

1. ingredients　　2. processes　　3. product　　4. rate
5. discovered　　6. lowered　　7. increased

Exercise 1

1. next　　2. yesterday　　3. frequently　　4. there

1. はじめに（First）油漏れのチェックをして、「次に」電源を入れる。
2. 車の新製品を見に行ったのは「昨日」。
3. ギターを弾いた頻度は「頻繁に」。
4. 友達が大阪に住んでいて、「そこに」（＝大阪に）会いに行きたい。

Exercise 2

1. exactly　　2. often　　3. especially　　4. rapidly

1. 「正確に、ちょうど」100 人がドローンのショーに参加した。
2. ホームセンターに買い物に行く頻度は「しばしば」。
3. 「特に」夏の川で泳ぐのが好き。
4. 病気が「急速に」広がったが、だんだんと減った。

Lesson 9

Review

(1) 1   (2) 2   (3) 4   (4) 1   (5) 3

訳

　ものをつなげることは、私たちの日常生活を向上させる方法だ。ものをつなげる例をいくつか見てみよう。

　1＋1 は 2 である。これは単なる計算だ。では、2 つの車輪を組み合わせるとどうなるだろうか。自転車になる！ 2 つのものを組み合わせると、それらは新しい形になる。

　青と黄色を混ぜると、緑になる。水素と酸素を結合させると水になる。これらの変化は、どのように 2 つの異なるものが作用して新しい状態をつくり出すかを教えてくれる。

　3 つ以上の異なるものを組み合わせることもできる。それぞれの単語の最初の文字を組み合わせることを考えてみよう——道具、電気、細胞、熱、ネットワーク、石油、光、操作、ガス、庭。

Lesson 10

Vocabulary

avoid	動　詞	（ 避ける ）
cause	動　詞	（ 引き起こす ）
experience	名　詞	（ 経験 ）
follow	動　詞	（ あとについていく ）
leave	動　詞	（ 出発する、残す ）
think	動　詞	（ 思う、考える ）
vivid	形容詞	（ 鮮明な ）

1. follow　　2. cause　　3. experience　　4. leave

5. avoid　　6. think　　7. vivid

Exercise 1

1. His vivid green hair surprised his friends.　　　過去分詞　surprised

2. A technical trouble caused the accident.　　　過去分詞　caused

3. A dance party follows the ceremony.　　　過去分詞　followed

4. Someone broke the window yesterday.　　　過去分詞　broken

Exercise 2

1. His friends were surprised by his vivid green hair.

2. The accident was caused by the technical trouble.

3. The ceremony is followed by the dance party.

4. The window was broken yesterday.

　　4. 動作主に注目しないので、by someone は不要。

Lesson 11

Vocabulary

attract	動　詞	（ ひきつける ）
compare	動　詞	（ 比較する ）
describe	動　詞	（ 詳しく説明する、描写する ）
empty	形容詞	（ 空っぽの ）
fill	動　詞	（ 満たす ）
improve	動　詞	（ 改善する ）
several	形容詞	（ いくつもの、様々な ）

1. describe　　2. improve　　3. fill　　　4. empty

5. attract　　6. compare　　7. several

Exercise 1

1. [Because] I didn't have time, / <u>my friend kindly helped me</u>.

2. <u>They bought the new EV</u> / [after] its driving system was improved.

3. <u>We have seven miles to go</u> / [before] we can take a break.

4. [While] the cat was sleeping on the tree, / <u>he painted its picture</u>.

💡[　　　　　]内の語句が従属節の目印

Exercise 2

1. I compared three smartphones / [because] I wanted to get the best one.
　 S　V

2. Bob was talking on the phone / [when] his friend suddenly opened the door.
　　S　　V

3. [If] your hands are empty, / will you carry this bag for me?
　　　　　　　　　　　　　　　　S　　V

4. Editors checked several facts / [before] the book was published.
　　　S　　　　　V

Lesson 12

Review

(1) 3　　(2) 1　　(3) Emma was encouraged　　(4) 3　　(5) 3

訳

　あるところに、エマというスポーツが大好きな女の子がいました。彼女は様々なスポーツに挑戦しました——テニス、バスケ、サッカー、水泳、マラソンもです。友達はみんなすごいねと言ってくれますが、エマは普通のスポーツでは物足りなくなってきました。新しい経験をしたいと思っていたのです。

　ある日、エマが友達と公園で遊んでいると、フリスビーを見つけました。彼女はそれを拾い上げると試しに投げてみました。するとそれは美しい放物線を描いて飛び、地面に落ちました。これすごく楽しい、と彼女は思いました。

　友達は彼女の投てきに感動して、フリスビーをどれだけ遠くまで飛ばせるか知りたがりました。エマが投げるたび、友達は距離を測って平均値を出しました。投てきがどんどん上手になるので彼女は嬉しくなりました。友達は、もっと練習しなよと彼女を励ましました。

　エマはフリスビーの腕を磨こうと決意しました。投てきの距離を予測するためには、投げるときの高さと角度に加え、様々なディスクの材料に基づいて考える必要がありました。そのため、彼女は投てきの練習に加え物理学を学びました。ついにエマはフリスビープレーヤー兼物理学者になり、みんなを感動させました！

Lesson 12 のパラグラフ構造

- Topic sentence 四角で囲ってある文
- Supporting sentences 間にある文
- Concluding sentence 下線の引いてある文

There was a girl named Emma who loved to play sports. She tried several sports—tennis, basketball, soccer, swimming, marathon. Her friends admired her, but she was getting bored with ordinary sports. She wanted a new experience.

One day, when Emma and her friends were playing in a park, they found a frisbee. She picked it up and threw it. It flew through the air in a beautiful curve before landing on the ground. She felt so good.

Emma's friends were impressed with her throw, and they wanted to know how far the frisbee could go. Every time she threw it, they measured the distance and calculated the average of her throws. She was happy to find out that her throws were getting better and better. Her friends encouraged her to practice more.

Emma was determined to improve her frisbee skills. She needed to predict the distance of her throws based on the height and angle of her toss and the various materials of the disc. So, she studied physics in addition to practicing throwing. Finally, she became a frisbee player who is also a physicist and impressed everyone!

動詞語形変化表

*が付いている単語は Vocabulary で出てきた動詞です。

原形	過去形	過去分詞形	現在分詞形
allow*	allowed	allowed	allowing
attract*	attracted	attracted	attracting
avoid*	avoided	avoided	avoiding
be	was, were	been	being
become	became	become	becoming
begin	began	begun	beginning
break	broke	broken	breaking
bring	brought	brought	bringing
build	built	built	building
buy	bought	bought	buying
call*	called	called	calling
catch	caught	caught	catching
cause*	caused	caused	causing
combine*	combined	combined	combining
come	came	came	coming
compare*	compared	compared	comparing
compete*	competed	competed	competing
consider*	considered	considered	considering
consume*	consumed	consumed	consuming
contain*	contained	contained	containing
cost	cost	cost	costing
defeat*	defeated	defeated	defeating
describe*	described	described	describing
develop*	developed	developed	developing
discover*	discovered	discovered	discovering
do	did	done	doing
draw	drew	drawn	drawing
drink	drank	drunk	drinking

原形	過去形	過去分詞形	現在分詞形
eat	ate	eaten	eating
estimate*	estimated	estimated	estimating
explain*	explained	explained	explaining
feel	felt	felt	feeling
fill*	filled	filled	filling
find*	found	found	finding
fly	flew	flown	flying
follow*	followed	followed	following
forget	forgot	forgotten	forgetting
get	got	got, gotten	getting
give	gave	given	giving
go	went	gone	going
grow	grew	grown	growing
have	had	had	having
hold	held	held	holding
improve*	improved	improved	improving
increase*	increased	increased	increasing
invent*	invented	invented	inventing
justify*	justified	justified	justifying
keep	kept	kept	keeping
know	knew	known	knowing
lead	led	led	leading
leave*	left	left	leaving
lose	lost	lost	losing
lower*	lowered	lowered	lowering
make	made	made	making
mean	meant	meant	meaning
meet	met	met	meeting
modify*	modified	modified	modifying
prepare*	prepared	prepared	preparing
put	put	put	putting
read	read	read	reading

原形	過去形	過去分詞形	現在分詞形
refuse*	refused	refused	refusing
replace*	replaced	replaced	replacing
rise	rose	risen	rising
run	ran	run	running
say	said	said	saying
see	saw	seen	seeing
set	set	set	setting
shake	shook	shaken	shaking
show	showed	shown	showing
sleep	slept	slept	sleeping
speak	spoke	spoken	speaking
spend	spent	spent	spending
stand	stood	stood	standing
take	took	taken	taking
teach	taught	taught	teaching
tell	told	told	telling
think*	thought	thought	thinking
understand	understood	understood	understanding
win	won	won	winning
write	wrote	written	writing

空欄には自分で調べた動詞を書き入れてみましょう。

100 Vocabulary List

【 Lesson 1 】

☐ ☐ ☐	advance	名詞	進歩
☐ ☐ ☐	career	名詞	経歴、職業
☐ ☐ ☐	consider	動詞	よく考える、熟考する
☐ ☐ ☐	contain	動詞	含む
☐ ☐ ☐	device	名詞	装置、道具
☐ ☐ ☐	find	動詞	見つける
☐ ☐ ☐	invent	名詞	発明する
☐ ☐ ☐	modern	形容詞	現代的な
☐ ☐ ☐	modify	動詞	修正する、改良する
☐ ☐ ☐	require	動詞	必要とする

【 Lesson 2 】

☐ ☐ ☐	annually	副詞	毎年、一年ごとに
☐ ☐ ☐	call	動詞	呼ぶ
☐ ☐ ☐	compete	動詞	競争する
☐ ☐ ☐	collect	動詞	集める
☐ ☐ ☐	defeat	動詞	破る、負かす
☐ ☐ ☐	distance	名詞	距離
☐ ☐ ☐	exhaustion	名詞	極度の疲労
☐ ☐ ☐	pay	動詞	払う
☐ ☐ ☐	prepare	動詞	準備する
☐ ☐ ☐	vehicle	名詞	乗り物

【 Lesson 3 】

☐ ☐ ☐	attend	動詞	出席する
☐ ☐ ☐	create	動詞	つくる、つくり出す
☐ ☐ ☐	directly	副詞	直接的に
☐ ☐ ☐	knowledge	名詞	知識
☐ ☐ ☐	related	形容詞	関係のある

【 Lesson 4 】

☐	☐	☐	allow	動詞	許す
☐	☐	☐	ancient	形容詞	古来の、古代の
☐	☐	☐	architecture	名詞	建築、建築物
☐	☐	☐	consume	動詞	消費する、消耗する
☐	☐	☐	exciting	形容詞	興奮させる、わくわくさせる
☐	☐	☐	Mars	名詞	火星
☐	☐	☐	population	名詞	人口
☐	☐	☐	quickly	副詞	速く、急いで
☐	☐	☐	replace	動詞	取って代わる、取り替える
☐	☐	☐	wooden	形容詞	木製の

【 Lesson 5 】

☐	☐	☐	construction	名詞	建設、建造
☐	☐	☐	during	前置詞	～の間に
☐	☐	☐	estimate	動詞	見積もる、概算する
☐	☐	☐	figure	名詞	数値、数量
☐	☐	☐	innovation	名詞	革新、イノヴェーション
☐	☐	☐	justify	動詞	正しいと証明する、正当化する
☐	☐	☐	means	名詞	手段
☐	☐	☐	survey	名詞	調査、査定
☐	☐	☐	system	名詞	装置、制度
☐	☐	☐	technical	形容詞	工業技術の、科学技術の

【 Lesson 6 】

☐	☐	☐	attention	名詞	注意、注目
☐	☐	☐	funeral	名詞	葬式
☐	☐	☐	genuine	形容詞	本物の
☐	☐	☐	incidentally	副詞	ところで、ついでながら
☐	☐	☐	involve	動詞	関係させる、巻き込む

【 Lesson 7 】

☐	☐	☐	combine	動詞	結合させる、組み合わせる
☐	☐	☐	contrast	名詞	対照、対比
☐	☐	☐	develop	動詞	発達させる、発展させる
☐	☐	☐	electronic	形容詞	電気の
☐	☐	☐	exhibition	名詞	展示、展示会
☐	☐	☐	explain	動詞	説明する
☐	☐	☐	form	名詞	形、姿
☐	☐	☐	mechanism	名詞	機械装置、仕組み
☐	☐	☐	refuse	動詞	断る、拒絶する
☐	☐	☐	solid	形容詞	固体の、固形の

【 Lesson 8 】

☐	☐	☐	discover	動詞	発見する
☐	☐	☐	exactly	副詞	ちょうど、正確に
☐	☐	☐	frequently	副詞	頻繁に
☐	☐	☐	increase	動詞	増える
☐	☐	☐	ingredient	名詞	成分、材料
☐	☐	☐	lower	動詞	下げる、おろす
☐	☐	☐	machine	名詞	機械
☐	☐	☐	process	名詞	過程、工程
☐	☐	☐	product	名詞	製品、生産物
☐	☐	☐	rate	名詞	率、割合

【 Lesson 9 】

☐	☐	☐	connect	動詞	つなぐ、接続する
☐	☐	☐	electricity	名詞	電気
☐	☐	☐	example	名詞	例
☐	☐	☐	oxygen	名詞	酸素
☐	☐	☐	wheel	名詞	輪、車輪

【 Lesson 10 】

☐	☐	☐	avoid	動詞	避ける
☐	☐	☐	break	動詞	壊す
☐	☐	☐	bright	形容詞	明るい
☐	☐	☐	cause	動詞	引き起こす
☐	☐	☐	cell	名詞	細胞
☐	☐	☐	experience	名詞	経験
☐	☐	☐	follow	動詞	あとについていく
☐	☐	☐	leave	動詞	出発する、残す
☐	☐	☐	think	動詞	思う、考える
☐	☐	☐	vivid	形容詞	鮮明な

【 Lesson 11 】

☐	☐	☐	attract	動詞	ひきつける
☐	☐	☐	compare	動詞	比較する
☐	☐	☐	describe	動詞	詳しく説明する、描写する
☐	☐	☐	emission	名詞	放出
☐	☐	☐	empty	形容詞	空っぽの
☐	☐	☐	fill	動詞	満たす
☐	☐	☐	improve	動詞	改善する
☐	☐	☐	reduce	動詞	減らす
☐	☐	☐	result	名詞	結果
☐	☐	☐	several	形容詞	いくつもの、様々な

【 Lesson 12 】

☐	☐	☐	calculate	動詞	計算する
☐	☐	☐	impress	動詞	感動させる、印象づける
☐	☐	☐	predict	動詞	予想する
☐	☐	☐	throw	動詞/名詞	投げる/投げること、投てき
☐	☐	☐	various	形容詞	様々な

著　者

関根　路代　日本工業大学共通教育学群
廣田　純子　日本工業大学共通教育学群
山中　章子　日本工業大学共通教育学群
吉田　要　日本工業大学共通教育学群

Step by Step　～英語ワークブック～

2023 年 12 月 10 日　第 1 版　第 1 刷　印刷
2023 年 12 月 20 日　第 1 版　第 1 刷　発行

著　者　関根路代　廣田純子
　　　　山中章子　吉田　要

発行者　発田和子

発行所　株式会社　学術図書出版社

〒113－0033　東京都文京区本郷 5 丁目 4－6
TEL 03－3811－0889　振替 00110－4－28454
印刷　中央印刷（株）